Samson

God's Rebellious Champion

PHYLLIS J. STEVENS

Andrew Kilcup
Illustrator

ILLUMIFY MEDIA GLOBAL
Littleton, Colorado

Samson

Copyright © 2021 by Phyllis Stevens

All rights reserved. No part of this book may be reproduced in any form or by any means—whether electronic, digital, mechanical, or otherwise—without permission in writing from the publisher, except by a reviewer, who may quote brief passages in a review.

Unless otherwise noted, all scripture is taken from the Holy Bible, English Standard Version®. ESV® Text Edition: 2016. Copyright © 2001 by Crossway, a publishing ministry of Good News Publishers. The ESV® text has been reproduced in cooperation with and by permission of Good News Publishers. Unauthorized reproduction of this publication is prohibited. All rights reserved.

The views and opinions expressed in this book are those of the author and do not necessarily reflect the official policy or position of Illumify Media Global.

Published by
Illumify Media Global
www.IllumifyMedia.com
"*Let's bring your book to life!*"

Library of Congress Control Number: 2021920086

Paperback ISBN: 978-1-955043-35-9
eBook ISBN: 978-1-955043-36-6

Typeset by Art Innovations (http://artinnovations.in/)
Cover design by Andrew Kilcup

Printed in the United States of America

Dedicated to my great-grandson, Paxton.

May you always have a heart to fully follow the Lord.

"You are the light of the world.
A city set on a hill cannot be hidden.
Nor do people light a lamp and put it under a basket,
but on a stand, and it gives light to all in the house.
In the same way, let your light shine before others,
so that they may see your good works
and give glory to your Father who is in heaven."

(Matthew 5:14-16 31:8 ESV).

Contents

    Foreword   6
    Preface   7
    Samson   11

1. The Angel of The Lord Visits Manoah and His Wife   12
2. Samson Goes Against God's Law   15
3. Foxes on Fire   22
4. Jawbone Height   26
5. The Missing City Gates   31
6. Evil Deception   34
7. The Powerless Samson   41
8. Samson's Revenge   46
9. Samson's Burial   49
10. Samson Teaches Us Two Things   51

    Epilogue: Overview of the Book of Judges   53

FOREWORD

Phyllis Stevens is a dynamic, committed, and enthusiastic lover of Jesus and His Word. The only thing that compares to that love is her love for her family, that is her husband, children, grandchildren, and church family. As long as I have known Phyllis, she has had a real and practical concern for what the Bible describes as "the fatherless", children needing the care and love of parents and of Jesus. This book is a product of that passion.

Writing about the story of Samson is a very courageous thing to do. He is a colorful and somewhat unique hero. His great passion was both a source of real trouble as well as great usefulness in God's service. He is included by name in Scripture's "hall of faith" in Hebrews 11. This book is written and illustrated in clear and compelling ways, causing us to think again about this unique Bible hero. Well done.

—Dr. Timothy Jordan, PhD

Preface

In order to understand the man Samson, we must look at Israel's history. The purpose of the book of Joshua in the Old Testament is to show how God kept His promises to Abraham and his descendants to give them the land of Canaan by a holy war. A holy war is one fought for religious reasons, not just for the purpose of one country ruling another. It was because of Canaan's sin that God was not pleased with them. This was not only a war about gaining land or power; it was a display of God's judgment toward the sin of the people of Canaan.

God is a fair God. He waited an exceptionally long time before he judged the Amorites, who lived in the land of Canaan. God saw that the Amorites had stubborn hearts and were not willing to repent and turn to Him. The Canaanites worshiped idols. They were also doing horrible things that the Lord hated in order to please their gods. One thing among many was that they sacrificed their children to the fire.

Because of all this, God kept the promise He made to Abraham by giving Israel the land of Canaan, and He also judged the Amorites for their sin.

Deuteronomy 9:5 says, "Not because of your righteousness or the uprightness of your heart are you going in to possess their land, but because

SAMSON

of *the wickedness of these nations* the Lord your God is driving them out from before you, and that he may confirm the word that the Lord swore to your fathers, to Abraham, to Isaac, and to Jacob" (emphasis added).

Joshua's Last Instructions to God's People Before He Died

- Be strong and always obey all that is written in the Book of the Law of Moses, do not turn away from it neither to the right hand nor to the left. (Joshua 1:7–8)
- Stay away from all heathen nations—nations that do not worship the one true God—and do not speak the names of other gods.
- They must continue to love God. It would be easy to stop loving God because their neighbors did not believe in the one true God. To continue loving God would require the Israelites to examine their hearts carefully.

Joshua Warned the People What Will Happen if Israel Stops Clinging to God

- God would no longer fight for them.
- The Canaanites would be like snares and traps, whips to lash them, thorns that fly back into their faces, stabbing their eyes.
- Miseries and troubles would increase until they perish from off this good ground that the Lord their God has given them.

PREFACE

SAMSON

Exodus 34:12–16 says, "Take care, lest you make a covenant with the inhabitants of the land to which you go, lest it become a snare in your midst. You shall tear down their altars and break their pillars and cut down their Asherim, (for you shall worship no other god, for the Lord, whose name is Jealous, is a jealous God), lest you make a covenant with the inhabitants of the land, and when they whore after their gods and sacrifice to their gods and you are invited, you eat of his sacrifice, and you take of their daughters for your sons, and their daughters whore after their gods and make your sons whore after their gods."

Israel forgot all of Moses' and Joshua's instructions. Knowledge or memory that does not change behavior is worthless. "For my people have committed two evils: they have forsaken me, the fountain of living waters, and hewn out cisterns for themselves, broken cisterns that can hold no water" (Jeremiah 2:13).

Samson

God used Samson to accomplish His purpose, even though Samson never lived like a true Nazirite until his later years. "Everyone did what was right in his own eyes" **(Judges 21:25).**

This is the first time the calling of God's judge had happened before their birth. The entire reason for Samson's birth was to deliver Israel.

1

The Angel of The Lord Visits Manoah and His Wife

Manoah and his wife were Danites. They were from the tribe of Dan. Manoah's wife was barren; therefore, they had no children. One day, the Angel of the Lord appeared to Manoah's wife and said, "You shall conceive and bear a son. So then drink no wine or strong drink, and eat nothing unclean, for the child shall be a Nazirite" (Judges 13:7).

A Nazirite was someone who was devoted or set apart for God's purpose. Numbers 6:1–6 tells us that a Nazirite could not drink strong or fermented drink. He could not drink grape juice nor eat grapes or raisins. He could not come into contact with dead bodies. All the days of his separation he shall be holy to the Lord. The angel also stated, "No razor shall come upon his head, for the child shall be a Nazirite to God from the womb, and he shall begin to save Israel from the hand of the Philistines" (v. 5).

THE ANGEL OF THE LORD VISITS MANOAH AND HIS WIFE

SAMSON

The name Nazirite means "to vow." A Nazirite vow was normally for a limited amount of time. Samson was different because his vow would be for life.

Manoah's wife was so excited. She immediately ran to her husband and said "A Man of God came to me. . . . [and] He said to me, 'Behold, you shall conceive and bear a son. . . . the child shall be a Nazirite to God from the womb until the day of his death" (v. 7).

Manoah fell on his knees and prayed with his wife for the Man of God to return and teach them how to bring up this child. The Angel of the Lord did return and repeated everything to Manoah that He had told his wife. When the Angel of the Lord finished speaking, Manoah sacrificed a young goat with a grain offering on a rock to the Lord. While the flames went up toward heaven from the altar, the Angel of the Lord arose in the flames that blazed up. When Manoah and his wife saw this, they "fell on their faces to the ground" (v. 20).

Judges 13:24 continues, "And the woman bore a son and called his name Samson. And the child grew, and the Lord blessed him." When Samson became a young man, the Spirit of the Lord began to stir in Samson. It was time for him to deliver Israel. Israel had become content to live under pagan domination. They had forgotten Joshua's warning. God's purpose for Samson was to cause a breach between Israel and the Philistines.

2

Samson Goes Against God's Law

Samson was raised by godly parents.

When he was a young man, he walked down to Timnah, which was around five miles from the area where he lived in Zorah. Timnah was under the control of the Philistines. There he saw a beautiful daughter of a Philistine and lusted after her.

Since marriage in those days was contracted by the parents, Samson went to his parents and insisted they get her to be his wife. In Judges 14, he said, "I have seen a woman in Timnah of the daughters of the Philistines. Go get her to be my wife." His parents said to him, "Is there no woman among your people, the Israelites? Why must you go and get a wife from the uncircumcised Philistines?" Samson ignored his parents and said to his father, "Get her for me, for she is right in my eyes" (Judges 14:3). His parents knew that his people, the Israelites, were expressly forbidden by Mosaic law to married anyone who does not believe in the one true God. Though Samson's parents objected, they still allowed him to marry the Philistine woman.

SAMSON

SAMSON GOES AGAINST GOD'S LAW

Manoah and his wife did not know that God would use this marriage to begin the breach between the Philistines and the Israelites. At this time, the Philistines had complete control over Israel.

This does not mean that breaking God's law was desired by God; instead, it means Samson's decision was overruled by God for His own purpose and glory.

Samson took his parents to Timnah to arrange the wedding between him and the woman. On the way there, as his parents walked ahead, Samson was attacked by a young lion near a vineyard. Seeing the roaring lion, the power of the Spirit of the Lord came mightily upon Samson as the lion lunged toward him, Samson caught the lion, wrestled it to the ground, and ripped it apart with his bare hands.

Samson caught up with his parents but did not tell them what he had done.

Once arriving into Timnah, Samson met and talked with the woman for the first time. She pleased Samson well, and both parents agreed to the betrothal. After the betrothal period was completed, Samson and his parents traveled back to Timnah for the wedding. When he reached the place where Samson had killed the lion, Samson discovered that a swarm of bees had made honey in the carcass of the lion. He stopped and scooped out some of the honey and ate it. It was sweet and refreshing. He scooped out more for his parents. When he reached them, he offered the honey as a refreshment. He did not tell his parents that the honey came from a dead lion's carcass, the one he had killed. He knew that touching the carcass of the dead lion violated his Nazirite vow.

After arriving, Samson continued to ignore his Nazirite vow. He hosted a traditional seven-day wedding feast where there was lots of food and riotous drinking. Servants brought out trenches of stale bread. Inside the bread were all types of meats, beans, and vegetables. Other servants kept the guest horns and bowls full of ale and wine.

After Samson's heart was merry from drinking too much wine, he said to the thirty bridegrooms who were the Philistines' guest, "Let me now put a riddle to you. If you can tell me what it is, within the seven days of the feast, then I will give you thirty linen garments, [large rectangular sheets, often used as undergarments], and thirty changes of clothes, but if you cannot tell me what it is, then you shall give me thirty linen garments and thirty changes of clothes" (Judges 14:12–13). This amounted to one from each of the guest.

The Philistines looked at each other and one said, "What is this riddle?" Samson replied, "Out of the eater came something to eat. Out of the strong came something sweet" (v. 14). Samson knew they did not know about the lion and the honey. Smiling, he continued enjoying the feast.

SAMSON GOES AGAINST GOD'S LAW

For three days, the Philistines met together and tried to solve the riddle. When they realized they could not solve it, they went to Samson's bride and threatened her and her family, saying, "Entice your husband to tell you what the riddle is, lest we burn you and your father's house with fire" (v. 15). She did not want to die or see her family harmed. Having to confront Samson unnerved her completely.

During the feast, Samson's wife said in a panicked tone, "You only hate me; you do not love me. You have put a riddle to my people, and you have not told me what it is" (v. 16). Samson turned to her, likely still eating his feast, and answered, "I haven't explained it to my father or mother, so why should I tell you?" His wife began crying. Every day when he saw her, she would cry and beg him for the answer to the riddle. Finally, on the seventh day of her tears, he told his bride the answer. Very relieved and happy, she hurried to the Philistines and explained the riddle.

The Philistines waited just before the sun went down on the last day of the feast, the seventh day, confident they had the answer, then yelled out to Samson: "What is sweeter than honey? What is stronger than a lion?" (v. 18). Now the Philistines were smiling and laughing.

Samson was furious because he knew his wife had told them the answer. He yelled out, "If you had not plowed with my heifer, you would not

SAMSON

have found out my riddle" (v. 18). By calling her a heifer, Samson was ridiculing his wife for her untamed stubbornness.

The Spirit of the Lord came mightily upon Samson. He angrily left the feast and went looking for a way to fulfill his obligation to the Philistines. In God's providence, He arranged for Samson to locate a camp of Philistines in the town of Ashkelon about twenty-three miles from Timnah.

This attack began the deliverance of Israel from the hands of the Philistines. Samson attacked and kills thirty Philistines and took their garments back to those who had told the riddle. He was furious!

To kill thirty Philistines was no small accomplishment. Numbers 14:27–33, tells us that ten spies told Moses they could not take the land of Canaan because it had strong, fortified cities and the people were giants who lived there. They told Moses, "We seemed to ourselves like grasshoppers, and so we seemed to them" (Numbers 13:33). The Philistines were inordinately tall. Samuel 17:1–51 tells us that the Philistine named Goliath was about nine foot nine. Goliath wore a bronze helmet and a coat of scale armor weighing around 125 pounds with bronze greaves, which protected the lower legs and thighs. He was also armed with a bronze javelin and a long spear with a fifteen-pound iron tip.

Samson returned to the wedding feast that was still going on and flung the garments at the thirty Philistines before returning home with his parent and without his wife.

SAMSON GOES AGAINST GOD'S LAW

Samson had failed to consummate the marriage. Therefore, her father, to avoid his daughter being disgraced in front of friends and family, gave his daughter to Samson's best man to marry. This would have been seen as an annulment, because Samson left without consummating the marriage.

3

Foxes on Fire

Months later, during the wheat harvest, Samson remembers his wife and takes a young goat to her as a gift. When he arrives, he says to the father, "Let me go into my wife's room." The father tells Samson that his wife has been given to another—Samson's friend, in fact! The father says, "I really thought that you utterly hated her, so I gave her to your companion. Is not her younger sister more beautiful than she? Please take her instead" (Judges 15:2). Samson was angry. He did not want the younger sister. Now he would unleash his anger on losing his wife.

He again vents his anger on the Philistines for their trickery. He went out and caught three hundred foxes. He took them to a grain field of the Philistines and held them so they could not bite him, then tied their tails together. He fastened a torch to the tail of each pair and set fire to each torch. Terror-stricken, the foxes ran wildly, crying into the grain fields of the Philistines. They ran in all directions to prevent themselves from run-

FOXES ON FIRE

SAMSON

ning into a fire that another pair of foxes had already set. But as they ran, they started more fires. The cries of the foxes filled the farmers' ears, blocking out any other sound. The fire and smoke could be seen for miles. The fire burned up all the dry grain that was ready to be harvested, as well as grain not yet harvested. The fire in its fiery spread to the Philistines' vineyards and olive groves. Samson had just destroyed the Philistines' three main crops.

When the Philistines saw what was happening, they were shocked and yelled, "Who has done this?" (v. 6). Trembling, the people who kept the fields said, "It was Samson, the son-in-law of the Timnite. He was angry because his father-in-law took his wife and gave her to a Philistine to wed."

When the Philistines heard that Samson had caused this massive destruction, they retaliated by going to the house of his father-in-law and setting the house on fire. Inside were Samson's wife, father, and family. Everyone in the house died.

Motivated again by revenge for what they did to his wife and her family, Samson said, "If this is what you do, I swear I will be avenged on you, and after that I will quit" (v. 7).

Samson went out and found a camp of unsuspecting Philistines. He attacked them and killed hundreds. God was again using Samson for His purpose to put a divide between Israel and the Philistines. God wanted Israel to remember His words: "Take care, lest you make a covenant with the inhabitants of the land to which you go, lest it become a snare in your mist" (Exodus 34:12).

After the great slaughter, Samson walked to a rock cave in Ethem, which was in Judah. He went inside to rest among his own people.

4

Jawbone Height

The Philistines followed Samson all the way to Judah. They made their camp outside of Lehi. The man of Lehi saw this large camp of over a thousand Philistines. They could only stare at them in horror. They had to do something quick. A group of them decided to go talk with the Philistines. After reaching their camp, one said, "Why have you come up against us?" (Judges 15:10). The Philistines answered, "We have come to arrest Samson, and to do to him what he has done to us. He killed a camp of Philistines."

When the Israelites in Judah heard the reason for the Philistines' show of force, they gathered three thousand of their men and went to look for Samson. Their plan was to siege him and turn him over to the Philistines. They found Samson on top of the rock of Etam. Samson knew why they had come. He knew the Philistines would come looking for him. The men of Lehi approached him cautiously. One of the men shouted, "Do you

JAWBONE HEIGHT

not know that the Philistines are rulers over us? What then is this that you have done to us?" (v. 11).

The Israelites had accepted the domination of the Philistines. They were a shadow of their former conquering selves. They were comfortable with the "new norm," which was never God's plan.

Samson replied, "As they did to me, so I have done to them" (v. 11). The man of Israel said to Samson because they were afraid of the Philistines, "We have come to arrest you, and deliver you over to the Philistines." Samson looked at the three thousand and said, "Swear to me you will not attack me yourselves" (v. 12). The man of Israel said they would not kill him. Samson came down from the rock and held out his arms so that they could bind them. Several men held him while others tied his arms and hands with new ropes. Not wanting to shed Israelite's blood, Samson let them surrender him to the Philistines.

As soon as the Philistines saw that Samson's hands were bound, they started shouting and running toward him. Before the Philistines could reach him, "the Spirit of the Lord rushed upon him" (v. 14). He broke the ropes like they were burnt flax, and they fell from his arms. The men of Lehi saw what was happening and ran. Enraged, Samson looked around to see what he could use as a weapon against so many Philistines and "found a fresh jawbone of a donkey" (v. 15). An old jawbone would have been too brittle

SAMSON

JAWBONE HEIGHT

and broken easily. This was perfect. He picked it up and swung that jawbone with God-given accuracy and killed one thousand Philistines.

Breathing heavily, Samson said, "With a jawbone of a donkey, heaps upon heaps, with the jawbone of a donkey have I struck down a thousand men" (v. 16). In other words, he was saying, "I have made donkeys of them and piled them in heaps." He looked around at all the dead bodies, then flung the jawbone away. The place where he used the jawbone was also significant: *Ramath-lehi*, which means jawbone height.

Sweating and exhausted, he looked to the heavens and cried out to the Lord that he was extremely thirsty, "You have granted this great salvation by the hand of your servant, and now shall I die of thirst and fall into the hands of the uncircumcised?" (v. 18). This is one of only two prayers that are recorded for Samson.

God miraculously answered Samson's prayer by splitting open the hollow place (which means rock or mortar) that was in Lehi, and water came rushing out of it.

This was not the first time God provided water out of a rock for His people. In Exodus 17, the children of Israel were in the desert and became very thirsty from walking and complained to Moses. God told Moses to take his staff and strike a rock, which allowed water to flow from it so the people could cross the Red Sea. Likewise, with Samson, out of the rock came water.

SAMSON

Samson drank, the water. "And when he drank, his spirit returned, and he was revived" (Judges 15:19). Samson called the place where the water came out of the rock En-hakkore (spring of the caller) because he cried out to the Lord and the Lord answered him.

5

The Missing City Gates

Samson walked to Gaza, one of the chief Philistine cities. Gaza was not only the largest of the chief cities it was also an important one because the travelers' routes from the desert joined the road from Egypt there. It was about thirty-five miles from his home in Zorah. Once in Gaza, he saw a prostitute and decided to stay the night with her. Samson's physical strength was unmatched except by his moral weakness.

The Gazite people saw Samson go in to be with her and told the Philistine warriors that Samson had come to their city and where he was staying. The warriors knew that Samson must pass through the gate of the city in order to leave, so they surrounded the gate and said, "Let us wait till the light of morning; then we will kill him" (Judges 16:2).

They settled in, planning to wait all night at the gate for Samson to leave the city. But Samson surprised them by leaving at midnight while it was still dark instead of in the morning. Seeing the warriors waiting at the gate increased his fury. When he reached the gate, he used his great

SAMSON

THE MISSING CITY GATES

strength to pull up the doors, which were sixteen feet tall, and the gateposts, which locked the gate. The warriors were so shocked watching him destroy their city gates that they stood frozen.

Samson put the gates on his shoulders and walked uphill for days until he reached the city Hebron, which is forty miles away. He then placed the gate doors and posts on top of a hill, facing Hebron.

By taking away the gate doors of Gaza, Samson insulted and humiliated the people by leaving their city unprotected.

6

Evil Deception

Over time, Samson met and fell in love with a beautiful Philistine woman named Delilah. Delilah lived in the Valley of Sorek. When the Philistines rulers heard that Samson was often seen visiting a woman in one of their cities, they sent spies to find out who this woman was. They were told her name was Delilah, so they started to devise a plot to capture Samson using Delilah.

The Philistines had five major cities: Gaza, Ashdod, Ashkelon, Ekron, and Gath. The rulers of these cities called for Delilah to be brought before them. They said to her, "Seduce him, and see where his great strength lies, and by what means we may overpower him, that we may bind him to humble him. And we will each give you 1,100 pieces of silver" (v. 5).

This was an exorbitant amount of money, equal to many thousands of dollars. Delilah walked away, determined to find out the secret of Samson's strength for the Philistine rulers. She knew this money would raise her status in Gaza.

EVIL DECEPTION

SAMSON

The next time Samson came to visit Delilah, she waited until he was relaxed, then passionately asked him, "Please tell me where your great strength lies, and how you might be bound, that one could subdue you" (v. 6). Samson smiled and said, "If they bind me with seven fresh bowstrings that have not been dried, then I shall become weak and be like any other man" (v. 7). After Samson departed from her, she hurried to the rulers and told them what Samson had told her. She also told them when Samson was returning.

Before Samson arrived, the rulers went to where Delilah was living and gave her fresh, green bowstrings. They helped her hide them in her house. When Samson arrived, she waited until he fell into a deep sleep before carrying out her plot to weaken him. She left him sleeping, then quickly retrieved the bowstrings from their hiding place and tied Samson with them. When she was sure the bowstrings were secure, she stood back and yelled, "The Philistines are upon you, Samson!" (v. 9). Samson jumped up from his sleep and immediately broke the bowstrings as if they were strands of yarn that had been weakened because someone had set fire to them. Delilah then knew this was not the secret of how he could be subdued.

She looked at the destroyed bowstrings on the floor, then at Samson, and said, "You have mocked me and told me lies. Please tell me how you might be bound" (v. 10).

EVIL DECEPTION

Samson took for granted God's blessing on his life and continued to tease her regarding where his strength came from. He replied, "If you bind me securely with new ropes that have never been used, then I will be as weak as any other man." The Philistines heard this and sent for new ropes and hid them where Delilah could find them. (They did not know that this had already been tried by his own people, the Israelites.) After a long day, Samson fell asleep, and Delilah used the opportunity to get the new ropes. She tied him up as tightly as she could. When the ropes were secure, Delilah yelled, "The Philistines are upon you, Samson!" (v. 12). Samson jumped up from his sleep and broke the ropes as if they were thin pieces of thread.

Delilah, with a disappointed look, said to Samson, "You have done nothing but mock me and tell me lies. Now tell me what is it that will bind you and make you like other men." Samson looked at Delilah's disappointed face and said, "If you weave the seven locks of my hair into the fabric on a loom, I will be like other men." Samson is beginning to play with the very thing that made him a Nazirite. By telling Delilah about his hair, he was edging closer to his real secret.

Delilah wasted no time. Once Samson fell asleep, she found her loom that held an unfinished tapestry and brought it into the room where Samson lay sleeping. She set it next to his head. She sat down and patiently wove all seven lots of his hair tightly into the fabric on her loom. When she

SAMSON

was finished, she stood up and said loudly, "The Philistines are upon you, Samson! But he awoke from his sleep and pulled away the pin, the loom, and the web" (v. 14). The fabric was torn from the loom, and the tapestry was destroyed. The loom lay on the floor in pieces. Delilah just stood there, staring at the destruction.

Delilah was frustrated, so frustrated that she did not realize her nails were cutting into the palms of her hands. She could see the money slipping away. Along with her beauty, she wanted power and status. She cried to Samson, "How can you say that you love me when you don't show it? You have made fun of me three times and told me nothing but lies."

Samson thought Delilah was teasing him, when she really was testing the success or failure of each method before she called the Philistines out of hiding.

Every day from that day on, she pleaded with him and begged Samson to tell her where his strength came from. When Samson's soul was vexed to death and could not take her nagging one day longer, he finally explained to her that he was a Nazirite and that his strength came from God. He said, "A razor has never come upon my head, for I have been a Nazirite to God from my mother's womb. If my head is shaved, then my strength will leave me, and I shall become weak and be like any other man" (v. 17).

EVIL DECEPTION

SAMSON

It was not the cutting of the hair that caused Samson's downfall; it was his disobedience and the fact that he never valued any of the Nazirite laws. He failed to view himself as someone special, a Nazirite from birth, set apart to be used by God.

When Delilah knew that he told her the truth, she started to plan her next steps to trap him.

She sent a message to the lords of the Philistines, saying, "Come up at once, for Samson has told me all his heart." The lords and Philistine warriors came quickly and brought with them the money they had promised her. Some of the warriors went quietly through the back door of Delilah's house and hid inside. The lords and the remaining warriors waited outside, out of sight.

Delilah sat down and rested Samson's head on her lap. She stroked his hair. Feeling comfortable, Samson fell into a deep sleep. As he slept, Delilah called for one of her male servants and told him to bring a sharp, short sword and shave off the seven locks of hair from Samson's head.

Because of Samson's foolish disobedience, Samson's strength left him while he slept.

Samson's long hair was the symbol of his special relationship with the Lord. It was a sign that he was not like any other men—a sign that God had chosen him for a special role. Samson put his relationship with Delilah above his relationship with the Lord.

7

The Powerless Samson

After the deed was done, Delilah very sure of herself this time, certain she'd found out his weakness, yelled, "The Philistines are upon you, Samson!" Samson awoke from his sleep, tragically not realizing that the Lord had departed from him. His hair was not his strength; the Lord was. When he saw the Philistines outside, he went out to fight them as before.

The powerless Samson was easily seized by the Philistines, who were hiding both outside and inside the house. They immediately gouged out his eyes, leaving him blind and even more helpless. They took him back down to Gaza, the place where Samson took the city gate. When they arrived in Gaza, they bound him with bronze shackles and threw him into a windowless, cold prison.

In prison, his job was to grind meal between two cylinder-shaped stones called a millstone, which in that day was a women's job. This was done to further humiliate Samson.

SAMSON

THE POWERLESS SAMSON

As time passed while Samson was in prison, his hair—the symbol of his Nazirite dedication—began to grow back.

The time came for the Philistines rulers to offer a great sacrifice to Dagon, one of their gods of grain. They believed that Dagon had delivered Samson into their hands. Thousands of people from all five cities started pouring into Gaza for the celebration. They gathered inside, outside, and on the roof the temple.

The ruler of Gaza stood up, looked around, and shouted to the people, "Our god has given Samson our enemy into our hand" (v. 23).

The people responded, "Our god has delivered into our hands our enemy. The destroyer of our land, and the one who killed many."

In 1 Samuel 4:12–18; 5:1–5, it states that Dagon, their god, had no power at all. During this time, the time of the Judges, the Philistines attacked Israel. When the Israelites saw they were losing the battle, Eli, along with the priest's sons, Hophni and Phinehas, sent for the ark of God to be brought to the battlefield. The Israelites did not realize God had departed from them because of their sin. They were using the ark of the covenant like a good-luck charm. During the battle, the Philistines captured the ark and took it to the temple of Dagon and set it at Dagon's feet to show that Dagon was more powerful than Israel's God.

The next morning when the people came to worship, they found Dagon had fallen over on the floor, in front of the ark, as if in submission to

SAMSON

THE POWERLESS SAMSON

Israel's God. The head and hands were broken off. The only thing that remained was Dagon's torso.

Israel's God is not only omnipresent (ever-present); He is omnipotent (almighty).

When the ruler's hearts were merry from too much ale and wine, they called for Samson to be brought up from prison. They wanted to mock Samson by making him entertain them. They wanted to see some of his acts of strength, perhaps him picking up massive logs and throwing them across the temple.

Samson was led into the temple by the temple guards. Because the Philistines had put Samson's eyes out, they did not fear his strength. After Samson had performed for the people, the guards called for a young boy who was watching Samson and told him to take Samson to stand next to the temple pillars until they were ready to take him back to prison.

8

Samson's Revenge

The Philistine temple was comprised of a long inner chamber with two major pillars supporting the roof. All the Philistine rulers and lords were inside the temple, and over three thousand men and women were on the roof of the outer court as they watched Samson.

Samson was leaning against one of the smaller pillars when he said to the young lad, who was standing next to him, "Let me feel the pillars that support the temple so that I may rest on them." The young boy led him to the two main supporting pillars. As he was leaning on the pillars, Samson, prayed to the Lord, "Oh, Lord God, please remember me and please strengthen me only this once, Oh God, that I may be avenged on the Philistines for my two eyes" (Judges 16:28). Samson calls on God, Elohim, God of power and might. He now knows that his strength is from the Lord.

Samson took hold of the two supporting pillars, braced himself, shifted his legs apart, and put his right hand on one pillar and his left hand on the other pillar, then prayed, "Let me die with the Philistines!" (v. 30).

SAMSON'S REVENGE

SAMSON

God granted his final prayer. Samson then pushed with all his might. The roof of the temple started to sway. People started holding on to each other and screaming. People panicked and started running, trying to find a way off the roof. As they were running, some tripped and fell and were trampled to death. Large stones fell on the rulers inside the temple, crushing them to death.

Samson killed more Philistines at his death than he did when he was alive.

God can use even tragedy and failure to accomplish His purposes.

9

Samson's Burial

Word spread fast that the temple had been destroyed and that Samson was dead. Samson's family heard what had happened to the temple and their brother Samson. His brothers gathered the whole family together and went down to Gaza to look for Samson's body.

When they arrived, they found the temple left in ruins and bodies scattered everywhere. They searched through the rubble until they found Samson's broken and bleeding body. With a heavy heart, his brothers picked him up and wrapped him in a blanket, laid him in a cart, and took Samson home for burial. They mourned the loss of their brother.

They buried Samson between Zorah (Samson's birthplace) and Eshtaol, in the tomb of Manoah, his father. This was the place the Spirit of the Lord first began to move in Samson's life.

This ended Samson's twenty years of judgeship over Israel. Though Samson had great ability and was gifted with great physical strength by the Holy Spirit, he gave in to temptation and suffered the consequences.

SAMSON

10

Samson Teaches Us Two Things

1. We Christian are the "salt of the earth" (Matthew 5:13). We serve as a preservative against the evils of society. During the time of Samson, the people had turned from the true God and began to worship other gods. The status quo was that "everyone did what was right in his own eyes" (Judges 21:25). Salt was a sign of God's covenant with Israel (Leviticus 2:13). Christians who are not totally committed to Christ have no eternal value.

2. God will use anyone and anything to accomplish His purpose. He used Samson, who never truly lived for God until the end of his life.

"I know that you can do all things, and that no purpose of yours can be withheld thwarted."

—Job 42:2:

Epilogue

Overview of the Book of Judges

Judges is named after a collection of individuals who led after Joshua's death. In this time of national decline, despite their promise to keep the covenant (Joshua 24:16–18), the people turned from the Lord and began to worship other gods. "Everyone did what was right in his own eyes" (Judges 21:25).

The elimination of the Canaanites from the land was both God's judgment on the Canaanites and a necessary action to keep Israel from being corrupted by their evil.

Israel compromised. They did not obey the Lord, and they did not drive the Canaanites out; instead, they made them into slaves. The tribe of Dan was forced into the hills out of their allotment of land God give them. This allowed the Canaanites to build a city called Luz, which was filled with idolatry in the *middle* of the promised land. Israel's incomplete disobedience meant it could no longer be a recipient of the promised blessings.

The people served the Lord all the days of Joshua and the elders who outlived Joshua.

This new generation had not seen the works of the Lord. They did not know the Lord or the works He had done. "And the people of Israel did what was evil in the sight of the Lord and served the Baals" (Judges 2:11). God's judgement: He would no longer drive out any of the nations Joshua left when he died.

By the end of the book of Judges, Israel is living in the midst of the Canaanites. They are intermarrying (Judges 3:6) with the Canaanites and serving their gods (Judges 3:7).

1. A pattern is repeated throughout the book:
2. The people abandoned the Lord.
3. God punished them by raising up a foreign power to oppress them.
4. The people cried out to God for deliverance.
5. God showed his mercy by raising up a deliverer.

By the time you get to chapter 13 in the book of Judges, the Israelites had accepted the domination of the Philistines. There is no mention of Israel crying out to God for help before God raises up Samson as a deliverer.

The heart of Israel's problem was a problem with Israel's heart.

The only way to know the one true God is through
His son, Jesus Christ.

John 3:16–17:
"For God so loved the world [you], that he gave his only Son, that whoever believes in him should not perish but have eternal life. For God did not send his Son into the world to condemn the world, but in order that the world might be saved through him."

Would you like to know
how the Israelites got into the land of Canaan? If so, then read
Joshua: A Warrior for God
by Phyllis J. Stevens